100 Little Lambs
WRITTEN BY SIERRA WILSON
ILLUSTRATED BY DANIKA RUNYAN
CFI • AN IMPRINT OF CEDAR FORT, INC. • SPRINGVILLE, UTAH

To my six little lambs,
I love you dearly.

—Sierra

ISBN 13: 978-1-4621-4643-7
ebook ISBN 13: 978-1-4621-4668-0

Published by CFI, an imprint of Cedar Fort, Inc.
2373 W. 700 S., Suite 100, Springville, UT 84663
Distributed by Cedar Fort, Inc., www.cedarfort.com

Library of Congress Control Number: 2023951495

Cover design and interior layout and design by Shawnda T. Craig

Printed in China

10 9 8 7 6 5 4 3 2 1

Printed on acid-free paper

"What man of you, having an hundred sheep, if he lose one of them, doth not leave the ninety and nine in the wilderness, and go after that which is lost, until he find it?

And when he hath found it, he layeth it on his shoulders, rejoicing.

I say unto you, that likewise joy shall be in heaven over one sinner that repenteth, more than over ninety and nine just persons, which need no repentance."

(Luke 15: 4-5 & 7)

One hundred lambs woke up with the sun.

One hundred lambs ready for fun.

They brushed their wool and curled their tails,

then washed in water from shiny, blue pails.

They polished their hooves and pranced in a line,

all of them fluffy and looking quite fine.

But where was Clover?

Ninety-nine lambs made chains out of flowers.

Ninety-nine lambs munched sweet grass for hours.

They spun in circles, twirling and dancing.

They skipped through meadows, leaping and prancing.

They fed baby birds and helped out a toad.

They always looked twice before crossing a road.

But where was Clover?

Ninety-nine lambs all done for the day.

Ninety-nine lambs so tired from play.

But where was Clover?

One little lamb had gone so astray.

One little lamb was lost far away.

She ran.

She dashed.

Thunder boomed.

Lightning crashed.

She stumbled.

She fell,

crying out

"Someone help!"

Then out from the rain came the Good Shepherd's hand.

He reached out to Clover and helped her to stand.

He hugged and held her right there in the rain.

"Hush, little one. I'll take all your pain."

One little lamb lifted up on strong shoulders.
One little lamb kept safe from sharp boulders.

She said, "Thank you, Good Shepherd,
for setting me free."

He said, "I love you, Clover.
You're so dear to me."

One little lamb carried
back to the sheep.
One hundred lambs so
joyfully leaped.

They followed the Shepherd
back into the fold.
Then snuggled together
away from the cold.

They offered up prayers
and nestled in tight.
They quietly snored in the
dark of the night.

One hundred lambs
all safe and asleep.

One Good Shepherd
watching over His sheep.

And there was Clover.